BHUTAN

BHUTAN

KINGDOM IN THE HIMALAYA

SANJAY ACHARYA

Lustre Press
Roli Books

*
For
Prabhakar, Mekhala & Mona
exceptional people who
passed by too soon…

*

ISBN: 81-7436-061-1

Fourth impression 2005
© **Roli & Janssen BV 1999**
Published in India by
Roli Books in arrangement
with Roli & Janssen BV
M-75, Greater Kailash II (Market)
New Delhi-110 048, INDIA
Ph.: ++91-11-29212271, 29212782
Fax: ++91-11-29217185
E-mail: roli@vsnl.com
Website: rolibooks.com

Text & Photographs:
Sanjay Acharya

Map:
Virender Kumar

Conceived and designed by
Pramod Kapoor at
Roli CAD Centre

Printed and bound in
Singapore

Monk plays the dranyen, *a
lute adorned with a dragon's
head and handcrafted in
wood and leather.*
Previous page 2: *The
Punakha Dromche festival
presided over by the Je
Khenpo, His Holiness
Trulku Jigme Choedar.*

Contents

*

Preface

It was the beginning of an adventure when in July 1980, with the monsoons breaking over New Delhi, my wife Sonya and I, along with tons of baggage and our golden retriever, boarded the Tinsukhia Express. Some thirty gruelling hours later, we were deposited unceremoniously on a dark platform at the New Jalpaiguri railway station. Rufus was worn to a frazzle having barked all the way at every passing train and animal, and Sonya was so benumbed by then that it made little difference to her where we had reached, as long as we were off the train. It was a relief to find Ugyen Norbu, a young photographer, who had come to meet us at the station, but it was still a long drive to Bhutan across the hot and dusty foothills of north Bengal.

For six more hours we bumped our way to Phuntsholing on pot-holed highways along a series of neatly pruned tea estates, until we passed under an arched gateway into Bhutan. Apart from the signboards and a number of policemen dressed in blue, it seemed no different from the crowded little towns we had hurried through on the way. And this was the mythical land which had so fired our imagination that we proposed to spend the next few years here! Greasy omelettes at the Kuenga Hotel—which offered both 'Fooding and Lodging'—didn't help our state of mind.

Five kilometres out of Phuntsholing, leaving behind the checkpost at Kharbandi, the atmosphere changed dramatically. The narrow highway wound its way up the hills blanketed by a thick mantle of dark green foliage. Giant ferns drooped from the slopes, and orchids and vines sheltered under the dense canopy of the tropical jungle. As we climbed higher, the temperature dropped steadily, and soon we were wrapped in the clouds. Peering through the swirling mist, the terrain looked even more dreamlike. Passersby were dressed in traditional Bhutanese attire, and even the architecture was different from anything we had seen before. It was another world we had entered, and we would come away transformed by it.

Communications were difficult in those days. Long distance telephone calls were almost impossible to connect and even telegrams took days to reach. There was no airline flying in and out of Paro, and the only way to get to Thimphu was to drive from the railway station at New Jalpaiguri or from the airport at Bagdogra in India. The 185 kilometres of winding highway from Thimphu to the plains took a little over five hours, but almost never became tiresome. Little excuse was needed to kick the Enfield motorcycle to life and ride the curves of the mountain road. One winter afternoon, after frozen pipes had deprived us of free-flowing water for a couple of days, Robert and Hootoksi astride their vintage Matchless and my Enfield set out on icy roads from Thimphu to Phuntsholing so we could get a hot shower!

Facing page: Guru Padmasambhava expresses benediction from the sacred thondrel unfurled from the ramparts of Wangdi Phodrang dzong before which a dancer leaps in celebration.
Following pages 8-9: Faith on the wind! Prayer flags flutter around a hillside chorten, spiritual sentinels overlooking the Thimphu valley.

Robert and Hootoksi Tyabji with their three boys, Michel, Farhad and Adil, and their black labrador, along with the two of us, made one big family. Thimphu was even more pastoral then with fewer cars on its streets. But it wasn't as quiet as we had imagined; if we weren't partying, there was a beeline to the bar at the Swiss Bakery. One quiet evening, however, the Tyabji's labrador went berserk throwing himself against the front door. Hootoksi opened the door, then banged it shut and stood transfixed, petrified, unable to move. Out on the balcony, a step from the door, lay a full-grown leopard!

Working with Robert on a UNICEF project to set up the Development Support Communication Division (DSCD) in Thimphu was a rewarding experience in itself. Incorporating the DSC activities as an integral component of the development process was an innovative step with far-reaching ramifications. Perhaps nowhere else had audio-visual support been accorded this pivotal role in national development, but it was seen in Bhutan as a catalyst to bring the benefits of social welfare, education, hygiene, nutrition and health care to a new generation.

Bhutan is an incredibly special place, and being there has been an experience of a lifetime. It seemed so idyllic, that it was almost inevitable that we should start a family. Our son, Nikhil, was born in 1981 at the Thimphu General Hospital at a time when any Bhutanese with the means would go abroad for the delivery. Sonya's mother, who had come all the way to Bhutan for the occasion, was compelled to urge carpenters and masons working in the makeshift labour room to take a break at least until the baby was born! It was a pleasure to reintroduce Nikhil to Bhutan in 1997 and show him his roots.

Several books have been written on Bhutan providing an insight into the life and culture of the people and illustrating the variety of landscapes of this wondrous land. Michael Aris' Bhutan: The Early History of a Himalayan Kingdom *and* The Raven Crown: The Origins of Buddhist Monarchy in Bhutan *make fascinating reading. In the 1980s, the bible for all visitors was G.N. Mehra's* Bhutan: Land of the Peaceful Dragon, *and I am fortunate to have an autographed copy on my shelf.*

While living in Bhutan in the early eighties, Sonya and I came in contact with Yoshira Imaeda and Françoise Pommaret who, along with Guy van Strydonck, published one of the finest picture books on Bhutan, A Kingdom of the Eastern Himalaya. *Tibetologist, historian and linguist, Françoise has since published several other books on Bhutan including an illustrated guidebook,* Buddhist Fort of the Himalayas. *More recently, she has contributed to and edited* Mountain Fortress of the Gods, *a truly significant work which presents the kingdom through the eyes of nine scholars, western as well as Bhutanese, and serves as a catalogue for a major travelling exhibition.*

Flowers of Bhutan *by Keiji Nishioka and Sasuke Nakao is the product of a lifetime of research into the ecologically unique ethnobotanical realm of the country. Bhutanese writers Karma Ura, author of* The Hero with the Thousand Eyes, *and Kunzang Choeden specialising in resurrecting the folk tales of Bhutan and writing on women's issues, are a new breed of intellectuals in Bhutan expressing themselves in the English language. I am greatly indebted to the scholarship of these works, and others too numerous to mention here, for the enlightenment they have given me.*

I have many friends in Bhutan whom I cannot thank enough for all their help and support. Dasho Benjy has always been accessible and warm in his welcome, and I have often looked to him for sage advice and counsel. He has amused and beguiled, and stimulated with his intense sharpness of mind. Dasho Meghraj is an old friend I can always count on. As Director-General of Posts and Telegraphs, he generously made available the philatelic bureau, and some of the images are presented in this book. Salman Haider, India's envoy to Bhutan in the 1980s, lent us the wisdom of his incisive and eclectic mind; and his wife, Kusum, brought a new dimension to our existence with the staging of the play, Rashomon.

Amongst my colleagues at DSCD, a lasting friendship has endured with Ugyen Wangdi, whose professional qualities I have respected and on whom I can always call upon to share his experiences of trekking and travelling in Bhutan—even more tempting

Jakar dzong *in Bumthang enveloped in swirling monsoon clouds.*

while sharing a home-cooked Bhutanese meal washed down with home-brewed arrah. Ugyen Norbu—Uncle Norbu to his friends—is unfortunately no longer with us, and I deeply miss his company in Bhutan. We revelled in the opportunity to make photographs and worked long hours together in the darkroom. He was always different, very cool and imperturbable, and Sonya and I had a wonderful trek with him up to Phajoding and the lakes of Jimilangtso.

Mingbo Drukpa and Kharga Bahadur Lama have been through thick and thin with us, and are part of our extended family. Friends at the Sambhara pub have constantly delighted with their good cheer and unfettered exchange of ideas, views and information.

I met George DeSerres first at the Sambhara and we have ever since shared a mutual love for flying, not to speak of computers and single malts. He has an interesting

perspective on Bhutan coming perhaps from his unique overview—from the cockpit of the BAe 146 which he pilots with such grace.

Our family in Bhutan are Robin Wangdi and Chhozom, who have always kept the doors of their home open for all of us. Robin extended the support of every facility at his command, and arranged every trip to perfection. His infectious sense of humour and well-meaning irreverence have kept us in fits ever since we first met in 1980, and the years have only sharpened his wit. Chhozom happily fed and sheltered us, and drove us where even Robin would not venture.

Bhabche and Dorje accompanied us on the arduous trek to Chomolhari, helped carry my gear, produced some of the most sumptuous meals in unbelievable

Base camp for the towering Chomolhari mountain at Jangothang. A caravan of yaks wait to be saddled for the arduous 'Snowman's Trek' across the Bhutanese Himalaya.

circumstances and made us as comfortable as possible. And there were many others who were my guides around Bhutan when I returned to work on the book.

I have to thank Bela Butalia for holding my hand through the extremely difficult and unfamiliar vocation of writing a book, and Pramod Kapoor for the opportunity to do it. Last, but not least, Sonya has been a wonderful companion on my trips to Bhutan, and I value her judgement on what this book should be—and could have been!

Facing page: *Prayer flags strung across the raging river Thinchhu below Tango monastery near Thimphu.*
Following pages 14-15: *Druk Air BAe 146 on final approach to Paro airfield with Rinpung* dzong *in the background.*

13

Chapter I

Touchdown

'**L**adies and gentlemen, in preparation for landing at Paro, please fasten your seat belts. Many of you must be familiar with flying over mountains, but this approach is a little unusual where you will see hills and trees and buildings quite close to the wing tips. Don't worry, this is normal procedure for Paro. The scenery is beautiful. Enjoy the ride!' That's George DeSerres from the flight deck of the Druk Air BAe 146 four-engine jet on final approach to Runway One-five. Vietnam vet, airplane jockey over the jungles of the Amazon and the Zambezi, and sporting a streaming white moustache, Captain George, as he is popularly known in Bhutan, is one of a handful of pilots around the world qualified to fly in and out of Paro airfield. It is evident that in this age of flying computers, he loves this seat-of-the-pants stuff, dodging in over the valley through a tiny window in the clouds, making a tight turn over the terraced paddy fields, sideslipping over Smith's House and lining up with the long black ribbon along the Paro river.

There is no airfield like Paro, and even for the passenger it's a magnificent flight coming in over the Himalaya with stunning views of some of the highest mountains in the world: Everest, dark and forbidding, towering above every feature on earth with Makalu and Lhotse for company; Kanchanjunga, blanketed in shimmering white and perhaps the most beautiful massif of them all; finally, Chomolhari, the 7,300 m (24,100 ft) dome-shaped, snowcapped summit in Bhutan. Then, low into the valley, wings rocking in the turbulence of mountain currents, banking over emerald fields, red chillies drying on black slate roofs, rushing white water in a swift-flowing stream, a mule train winding its way along a bridle path, and there it is: the Paro Dzong, a majestic fortress and monastery dominating a pine-forested hillside. Moments later the 146 greases in the smoothest landing you ever experienced.

Out on the tarmac, the brisk mountain air perks up my senses. Paro is bathed in a brilliant glow as the late-afternoon sun streams in through a filter of just-passing storm clouds, still warm despite a chill breeze gusting now and again from the south where the valley narrows into a windswept funnel as far as its confluence with the river Wang which meanders down from the capital, Thimphu. Life in a village across the perimeter fence continues as always, unperturbed by the swooping aircraft and whine of jet engines. Smoke from a cooking fire curls up from the window of a large mud house, its rafters blackened but its walls painted a neat white. Slivers of yak meat are let out to air-dry in the wood smoke. On a freshly mud-plastered patio, a group of women dressed in traditional *kiras* stand winnowing the harvest which has just begun. Boys herd the family pigs. An archery contest is underway along the river on a field lined with poplars accompanied with song and dance and the occasional war-whoop of triumph as an arrow thunks into its mark on a metre-high white board.

Facing page: Drummer of Dramitse at Wangdi Phodrang.

The railway journeys of the past, followed by the long drive into the Bhutanese heartland somehow prepared the visitor to expect the unfamiliar. But it's somewhat unnerving to be transported into this amazingly different world without a significant time transition.

Bhutan is a country like none other. Secluded in the mountain fastnesses of the eastern Himalaya, quietly tucked away between the sultry riverine plains of India and the cold and arid Tibetan plateau, this tiny kingdom has managed until quite recently to remain supremely aloof from the rest of the world. Perhaps because of this insularity, Bhutan has retained its allure as the last Shangri-La with its breathtaking landscapes of snow-clad mountains and verdant valleys, deep forests and rushing streams, and its ancient heritage of Mahayana Buddhism and Tantric spirituality. No bigger than

Capt. George DeSerres in command of Druk Air's BAe 146.

Switzerland but sparsely populated, Bhutan combines a heady mix of the medieval and the modern, of exquisite natural beauty and enchanting cultural traditions.

Bhutan is rich in flora and fauna. Ancient Tibetans referred to it as *Lho Jong Men Jong,* 'The Southern Valleys of Medicinal Herbs', and *Lho Mon Tsenden Jong,* 'The Southern Mon Valleys where Sandalwood Grows'. Rare orchids, herbal and medicinal plants, and wildlife thrive in its pristine environment. A fascinating range of ecosystems stretches across the space of a few kilometres. Steamy, tropical jungles of the foothills reverberate with the calls of the tiger, leopard and elephant while the unique golden langur shares the tall forest canopy with the great Indian hornbill. Temperate forests of oak, pine and rhododendron give way to Himalayan meadows aglow with blooming wild flowers. These are the haunts of the elusive snow leopard and the colourful tragopan, blue sheep and takin, Bhutan's national animal. Trek up to the base camp of the sacred Chomolhari mountain or even farther north, on the tough 'Snowman's Trek', for stunning views of Kula Kangri (24,700 ft) and Gangkar Punsum (25,000 ft), the tallest mountains in Bhutan, then down to the clover-shaped valleys of Bumthang in central Bhutan, a region renowned for its hand-woven textiles, fruit orchards and dairy products.

Predominantly agricultural, the valleys of Bhutan are blessed with fertile soils irrigated by streams and rivers fed perennially by melting glaciers and monsoon rains which roll in, black and thundering, from the Bay of Bengal. Terraced paddy fields paint the valleys a lush green in the summer while, in springtime, apple and cherry blossoms bring a riot of colour to the hills. In the higher reaches, barley and buckwheat are better suited to the colder climate and brilliant shades of amaranth ripen under the autumn sun. Water buffaloes plough the fields, women winnow the

Mount Everest from Flt KB-114 en route to Paro.

grain in wicker baskets, while the menfolk thresh the harvest. It's back-breaking labour even though it's made light of with song and dance and good humour. But it's picture-perfect!

Buddhism permeates every aspect of society in this mountain kingdom and is an integral part of everyday life. Red-robed monks preside over religious ceremonies which might have as much to do with celebrating weddings and births and the consecration of monasteries as with exorcising spirits from village homes, appeasing the rain gods, or simply welcoming a traveller. Old men and women, bent over their prayer wheels, circumnavigate a *chorten* and chant the Buddhist mantra, *Om Mani Padme Hum*—Hail

Following pages 20-21: *His Holiness the Je Khenpo, Trulku Jigme Choedar, Chief Abbot of Bhutan, watches the ritual* tsechu *dance from his chambers at the Tashichhodzong in Thimphu in the company of other lamas and royalty.*

to the Jewel in the Lotus. Clusters of colourful prayer flags, strung vertically from wooden poles, flutter incessantly from mountain ridges and from monasteries and fortresses where the heady smell of burning incense wafts through their time-worn portals.

Periodically, the sublime serenity of the monastery is shattered by the sound of clashing cymbals, bellowing trumpets and thundering drums as monks and laymen wearing demonic masks perform ritual dances to appease the guardian deities of Bhutan and bring blessings upon the onlookers. These festivals or *tsechus* are held throughout the year attracting people from distant hamlets who come dressed in their finest silk brocades and traditional dresses.

In Bhutan, men wear the *gho,* which may be loosely described as a cross between

A bamboo bow flexes to its limit to wing an arrow to its target at an archery contest in Thimphu.

a kilt and a kimono, made of hand-woven tartan fabric. The gown is tied at the waist with an embroidered cloth-belt or *kera.* Within the folds of the working man's *gho* will be the inevitable *bangchu* (bamboo basket) of food, a gourd of water or *chhang* (rice beer) and a large flat knife, very effective for hacking one's way through thick undergrowth and dense foliage. The *gho* is also an excellent receptacle for camera bodies and lenses for the working photographer! Garments made of heavy embroidered silk, traditional hand-crafted woollen boots and a long silver sword in an ornate scabbard worn at the side make up the attire of the aristocracy. At public functions or before entering a *dzong* (fortified monastery), common folk drape a white scarf or *kamne,* while the nobility—*dashos*—are privileged to don red scarves. Ministers are distinguished by their orange scarves and members of the National Assembly wear blue. Only the king and the Je Khenpo, the revered Chief Abbot of Bhutan, may wear

22

yellow. Women wear the *kira,* an elegant long dress held up with silver brooches at the shoulders and tied at the waist by a belt. Usually made of hand-woven and embroidered wool or cotton, silk *kiras* are in vogue at festivals and functions.

Tsechus usually take place in the courtyards of the great *dzongs,* which are the centres of government and religion in each district of the kingdom. Centuries old repositories of priceless treasures and works of art, these imposing structures have been built on ancient principles of architecture incorporating sun-baked mud blocks, stone and wooden beams and, traditionally, no metal—not even a nail—is used in the construction. Thick, slanted walls tapering inwards are whitewashed with a band of red painted across the top. Windows are unmistakably Bhutanese, with an arch on top and painted with floral or geometric motifs. Even ordinary Bhutanese homes

Monks blow horns and trumpets from the rooftop of Punakha dzong during the annual Dromche festival.

are unique in their design and construction, and very well suited to local lifestyles. Most of the houses are built on a rectangular floor plan, with steep wooden ladders reaching up through dark hallways to the well-lit upper floors which are constructed as open wooden frameworks. The family rooms and altars are situated here while the rest of the large barn-like house accommodates servants and guests, or where handlooms might clack through the day weaving exquisite patterns in home-spun wool. Roofs made of wood or slate and pitched above a flat floor, are held in place by rounded pebbles or heavy stones and coloured bright with chillies or corn left out to dry in the warm summer sun. Bundles of hay are stacked between the rafters, and slivers of meat strung out to be cured in the wood smoke of the kitchen fire.

History and religion are interwoven in Bhutan. *Druk Yul,* the indigenous name for

Bhutan is derived from Drukpa, the dominant religious sect of Mahayana Buddhism. Legend has it that Tsangpa Gyare Yeshe Dorje (1161-1211) was consecrating a new monastery in Tibet when he heard the sound of thunder. Taking it to be the call of a dragon, he named his monastery *Druk* and his school of religious thought came to be known as Drukpa. When Bhutan was unified by the Drukpa followers, *Bhotanta*—'the realm at the frontiers of Tibet'—became known as *Druk Yul,* 'Land of the Thunder Dragon'. Bhutan's national flag is emblazoned with the fire-breathing dragon, and the word *Druk* now embellishes almost every commodity in Bhutan, from bottles of jam and ketchup to the national airline.

Buddhism spread across the formidable Himalayan barrier to Tibet and beyond to China and Japan from its origins in Gaya, India, where the Buddha attained

Fearsome deity, dagger in hand, steps forth to vanquish the forces of evil.

enlightenment in the sixth century BC. Buddhism was first introduced in Bhutan in the seventh century AD when the Tibetan king, Songtsen Gampo established temples at Kyiuchu in the Paro valley and at Jampey in Bumthang. In the eighth century, the legendary saint, Padmasambhava, a wandering tantric from the Swat region in the North West Frontier mountains of present-day Pakistan—known widely as Guru Rinpoche—brought the teachings of Mahayana Buddhism to Bhutan. His eight manifestations, representing the Noble Eight-fold Path preached by the Buddha, are worshipped in temples throughout the kingdom, and Guru Padmasambhava is recognised as the father of the Nyingmapa sect, which is linked with Tantric Vajrayana Buddhism—the Vehicle of the Thunderbolt.

Facing page: *Homespun backpack for the new generation. A mother carries her child to the Paro festival.*

In the middle ages, Bhutan faced religious strife, regional conflict and incursions from Tibetan marauders, but eventually, in the seventeenth century, the Shabdrung Ngawang Namgyel, a lama of the Drukpa school, won a crucial battle against the Tibetans and managed to unify the country. Government and religion remain closely linked, even interwoven into the fabric of Bhutanese history and society. To this day, the king combines both religious and temporal powers—manifest in the double-edged tantric symbol of the Vajrayana—even though religious affairs have long been the preserve of the Je Khenpo.

While the two streams, Nyingmapa and Drukpa, have in the past touched off sectarian wars, the present dynasty traces its ancestry to both Guru Rinpoche and the Shabdrung. In the late nineteenth century, the *Penlop* of Tongsa established his

A commemorative stamp issued at the time of King Jigme Singye Wangchuk's coronation in 1974 depicts the raven crown of Mahakala.

supremacy and was elected the first king of Bhutan in 1907 by an assembly representing the monastic community, civil servants and village elders. His Majesty Jigme Singye Wangchuk, the fourth in the lineage to wear the Raven Crown, is the *Druk Gyalpo*—Dragon King—and rules supreme over *Druk Yul*, the Kingdom of the Thunder Dragon. The fact that Bhutan is governed by a monarchy vested not only with absolute temporal powers but with divine rights as well enhances its mystique.

As ancient and other-worldly as Bhutan undoubtedly is, there is also a tremendous sense of youthfulness and vigour. King Jigme Singye Wangchuk acceded

Facing page: *His Majesty King Jigme Singye Wangchuk at the National Day celebrations at Mongar.*

to the throne at the age of seventeen in 1974, and even today, young courtiers and administrators, many of them graduates from foreign universities, lend a fresh outlook emanating from Tashichhodzong. It is really no accident that Bhutan runs an efficient government devoted to development and conducts a sophisticated foreign policy overseas. Even the present Je Khenpo brings a sense of youthfulness to his high office.

While the young king ruled his country with a degree of wisdom beyond his years, he did not eschew his love for sports. It was always a pleasure to spend an afternoon watching him play basketball at Changlimithang in Thimphu with the sleeves of his *gho* tied around the waist. Very little could deter His Majesty from his game—not rain, not cold, nor even a high-level delegation visiting the capital.

Dasho Benjy exults as his arrow finds its mark at an archery contest.

Archery was everyone's preoccupation over the weekends, and the king would customarily host a luncheon at the palace grounds on the banks of the Thinchhu overlooking the Tashichhodzong. Both the teams would be accompanied by a posse of attractive cheerleaders who danced enticingly, sang suggestive songs and made lewd comments in an effort to distract the opposition, especially in the crucial moments before an arrow was let loose. Voodoo, much feared and often practised, would drive rival teams underground in the days before a tournament. It became known once that an attempt had been made to hex the royal team and, annoyed, the king meted out punishment as a prefect would in a public school: spend the weekend cutting grass on the palace lawns!

Always present at the archery contests was Dasho Paljor Dorji, a close confidant of the king. Now Minister for Environment, Dasho Benjy, as he is popularly known, was then CJ—Chief Justice and Court Jester—rolled into one unforgettable character. On one memorable occasion, he took over from the bandmaster and expertly swinging the long silver mace, led the royal pipes and drums a merry dance around the palace lawns before directing the entire contingent to a soggy end in a pond as spluttering bagpipes and muffled drums tried gamely to continue harmonising.

Benjy's antics were legendary. In the quiet ante-room of the Royal Chambers one morning, while His Majesty was engaged in private discussions with a visiting dignitary, CJ bet a senior minister a hundred Ngultrum that he could touch the chandelier overhead. He did—and won. At another time, he challenged the champion of the high beam to a pillow fight and, tricking him with the simplest of ploys, sent him tumbling into a mud pit below—in full view of his king.

When meeting the *Druk Gyalpo,* it is customary to bow and lay down one's scarf before him. Looking into the eyes of the Dragon King is simply not done—a particularly difficult imposition for the photographer. In deference to custom, I would take the picture, then lower my eyes. Difficult situations were closely avoided when, driving on serpentine mountain roads, the royal motorcade suddenly appeared around

His Majesty the King is all concentration as he pulls on a spring bow.

a blind corner. Bhutanese drivers would swerve to a halt against the hillside, and even before stopping, instinctively duck under the dashboard. Not only can one not look His Majesty in the eye, one cannot also be seen to be above him!

The King's sharp, penetrating eyes would search my soul when he looked at me. "Oy, Sangay!" he once beckoned, "Come, join in". His Majesty was dancing the *Lebe Lebe,* the climax to the 1980 National Day celebrations in Mongar in eastern Bhutan. Flattered, I joined the circle of dancers and tried to emulate the steps as best as I could while my cameras clashed and jangled around my neck and the lenses threatened to slip out of my gho! It's one picture I didn't get, but it was nevertheless a very special moment to be cherished forever.

Following pages 30-31: *Fertile valleys of Druk Yul. Paddy ripens on terraced fields dominated by the Chime Lhakhang monastery between Punakha and Wangdi Phodrang.*

Chapter 2

Environment & Development

An old woman, her face deeply wrinkled with time but wearing the beatific smile of a young girl smitten with love, looks up in adulation at the young man standing before her. He bends down to pour a drink of rum into a cup held in her outstretched, calloused hand, but she has eyes only for him. The king of Bhutan wades through crowds of village folk. He speaks to them, discusses their problems and immediately directs members of his retinue to address the issues. He serves his subjects some drink, some food, and distributes clothing and money to the needy, symbolising his greater mission of service to his kingdom.

This is Mongar in December 1980. His Majesty Jigme Singye Wangchuk is camping here with his entourage to celebrate the National Day, commemorating the elevation in 1907 of Ugyen Wangchuk as the first king of Bhutan. Mongar's tiny population has swollen ten-fold as thousands of people from distant villages and remote districts have gathered to see the *Druk Gyalpo*. For many, Mongar is their first taste of the 'big city', and even the sight of an automobile is a novelty. The east-west highway across central Bhutan passes through this little town but is yet to be paved, and a trail of dust rises in the wake of every passing car. The king arrives in a sleek Mercedes Benz S-Class sedan as *Pachham* dancers precede the royal motorcade leading to the venue of the public celebrations. Crowds throng the open arena. Men and women, families, children and the elderly mill about for a vantage position, but a hush descends as the king addresses them over the public address system. The policies enunciated at Mongar in fact marked a historical turning point in Bhutan's move towards modernisation with the monarch abrogating some of his powers in favour of regional authorities.

At the time, the king made it a practice to travel to different parts of the country to assess his people's needs and to fabricate a comprehensive agenda for development. For that reason, the National Day celebrations were held at a different place each year, and always the more remote districts of the country were favoured. The king made it a point to look into grassroots issues such as community health care, nutrition, hygiene, safe drinking water supply and primary education. In the meanwhile, the government began acquiring monastic lands to subsidise the clergy, and some of this property was allocated to landless peasants. Most significantly, the king initiated discussions with local administrators, community leaders as well as with his Council of Ministers to decentralise authority and to devolve power to the district *(dzongkhag)* and block *(gewog)* levels. This was no flash-in-the-pan populist gesture, but a well-considered measure designed to streamline the administrative machinery in the country, stimulate the development of local institutions and foster community responsibilities. The monarch's visit to the far-flung districts helped focus attention on these areas,

Facing page: Education is the springboard for Bhutan's development. Children on their way to the Dechenchoeling Primary School near Thimphu.

contributing towards achieving equitable and balanced development across the country. According to Karma Ura, author and civil servant in the Ministry of Planning, 'The objective of balanced development provides for equitable services and infrastructure throughout the country. The aim is to avoid the emergence of backwaters, as more and more parts of the country are brought into the economic mainstream.'

This process of modernisation was set in motion during the reign of Jigme Dorji Wangchuk who ruled for twenty years from 1952 until his sudden death in Nairobi in July 1972. India's first Prime Minister, Jawaharlal Nehru who trekked upto Paro in 1958 along with his daughter, Indira Gandhi, became an ally in the task of modernisation and economic development of Bhutan 'as an independent country, choosing (its) own way of life and taking the path of progress according to (its) will'. Nehru added, 'We are members of the same Himalayan family and should live as friendly neighbours helping each other.' The Chinese invasion of Tibet in 1954 had given Bhutan a rude shock, and the king realised it was time to emerge from years of splendid isolation to face the real world. But the task of modernisation was complex. It wasn't simply a question of finances; there were no technicians, engineers, doctors, teachers nor even skilled workers. Nehru readily agreed to assist Bhutan in its programme of planned economic development, and the gradual process of change began to take shape. In 1961, Bhutan embarked on its first five-year plan of development, with infrastructural expansion in road-building, telecommunication, education and manpower training being accorded the highest priority.

But the nature of change was going to be determined by the Bhutanese, and no doubt there was considerable opposition in the country to the idea of change itself. Over the next decade, Jigme Dorji Wangchuk made his reputation as the Father of Modern Bhutan, pioneering the process of democratisation and liberalisation of a traditionally despotic monarchy. It was a radical move, but intended to be introduced gently so as not to disturb the cultural ethos of the people. A High Court and National Assembly—*Tshogdu*—were set up, laws codified and serfdom abolished. The king voluntarily surrendered his power of veto and the laws passed by the Assembly were declared supreme. Upon his untimely death, the seventeen-year old Crown Prince who had earlier been appointed Penlop of Tongsa, ascended the throne, although the formal coronation took place two years later in 1974. His Majesty Jigme Singye Wangchuk assumed his father's mantle of bringing about social change and economic development while preserving Bhutan's ancient traditions, heritage and cultural identity.

In a far reaching step which could herald the winds of change, King Jigme Singye Wangchuk dissolved his nominated cabinet of twenty-two members and on 29 June 1998, put forward a package of reforms before the National Assembly in the form of a royal edict of *kasho*. The Tshogdu would henceforth be asked to ratify by secret ballot the appointment of six ministers and elect six new members to the Royal Advisory Council. Along with a royal nominee and two others appointed by the clergy, the fifteen members would form the King's cabinet and remain accountable to the National Assembly. The Assembly has however been left aghast by the King's proposition that the reigning monarch would have to win a periodic vote of confidence from the house and could even be asked to abdicate. Virtually unheard of in the annals of history for a monarch, particularly one enjoying absolute and divine powers, to voluntarily dilute his authority, this historic step reiterates the extraordinary relationship that exists between the King and his people. Members of the National Assembly, overwhelmed by the gesture, wept openly and requested His Majesty to revoke the *kasho*. But the *kasho* remains, and the Dragon Kingdom begins an intriguing journey into the next millennium. In setting out to build a post-modern, post-industrial, environment-friendly society, emphasis is placed on achieving self-reliance based on the development of communications, health care and education, improvements in agricultural and forestry practices and tapping the considerable resources of timber, minerals and hydroelectric power. However, material growth remains subservient to the spiritual enhancement of the people, and while Bhutan may be listed amongst the poorer nations of the world in terms of GNP, the kingdom is largely self-sufficient with little evidence of economic deprivation. The pursuit of *Gross National Happiness* is meant to take conscious precedence over achieving higher Gross National Product!

In choosing to travel the middle path and not driven by the lure of capital nor by

King Jigme Singye Wangchuk personally serves his subjects gathered at Mongar.

political opportunism, Bhutan has taken the route which balances the arguments for both environmental conservation and economic development. Even as the economy is dependent to a great extent on the exploitation of natural resources, emphasis is laid on the sustainable use and conservation of the environment. The Royal Government has been quick-footed enough to change tack as the situation demands and steer away from disaster. The 1980s witnessed a sudden spurt in deforestation. State-of-the-art technology was imported, often at the behest of international consultants, to extract timber which resulted in large tracts of virgin forests being hauled away to feed plywood board factories at Gedu and elsewhere in the lower reaches. But the lessons were quickly learnt, and following the scaling down of forestry operations, the factories were dismantled. The environmental upheaval around the 336-megawatt Chukha hydropower project has also been rectified and afforestation in the area has stabilised the ecosystem.

Conservation is an intrinsic part of the Buddhist ethos which has helped preserve

Bhutan's natural environment for generations. The Royal Government has made it quite clear that it values the ecological value of forest cover over revenue generation and has enacted far-reaching legislation such as the Forest and Nature Conservation Act, 1995, to safeguard its natural heritage. The state-run Forest Development Corporation has been granted monopoly rights over logging to ensure that felling is controlled and forest resources are not overexploited. The science of forestry too, has undergone a change with the philosophy of conservation given preference over the technique of exploitation. This has shown dividends in the overall increase of forest cover over the past decade. Significantly, afforestation has mainly been done with indigenous species closely approximating the original tree cover of the region rather than with exotic quick-growing varieties which have less social and ecological value. Today, Bhutan can boast of seventy-two percent cover of mostly virgin forests. This is particularly heartwarming in the South Asian context where environmental degradation has been widespread and conservation of natural resources has been put on the back-burner of political agendas.

Bhutan's forests are rich in biodiversity and its ecosystems are gene banks of global importance. Very few places on earth are endowed with such a variety of flora and fauna, and these have been effectively protected by the 1974 Notification on Reserve Forests and Wildlife Sanctuaries. The National Environment Commission of the Royal Government, headed by Dasho Paljor J. Dorji, Deputy Minister for Environment, has been instrumental in designating some 4,200 sq kms of pristine wilderness areas in northern Bhutan as a man-and-biosphere reserve. Appropriately named after the late King Jigme Dorji, the National Park is the habitat of a number of animal and plant species which are on the endangered list of CITES and IUCN, but are in good health in Bhutan. Many species are endemic to Bhutan and not found elsewhere. Some fifty varieties of rhododendron alone are seen in the kingdom, and several flowers and insects have yet to be identified. A good indicator of the environmental situation is that while in recent years the annual arrival of migratory black-necked cranes from Central Asia has been declining alarmingly at nesting sites in India and Nepal due to loss of habitat and disturbance, their numbers have risen significantly in Bhutan.

Biodiversity is found in agriculture too, where traditional farming techniques and multiple cropping have been the norm using organic methods of cultivation. The continued existence of species diversity and varietal diversity within species is a result of traditional cultural practices and knowledge systems. For instance, rice is not just food for people; its straw provides food for animals and the soil, while inter-cropping legumes with grain is both ecologically and nutritionally a sound practice. Single output measurements, as practised in green revolution terms, distort the full potential of different species with multiple yields in diverse farming systems, and hopefully the folly of cultivating hybrid monoculture crops will be discouraged. In Bhutan, where biomass output is high, Gross *Nature* Product could well be taken into account as an asset when computing Gross National Product.

Over the past few years, steps have been taken to improve community health care and primary education in Bhutan. Immunisation programmes have helped prevent several childhood diseases, and the Under-5 mortality rate (U5MR) has decreased from a high of 300 per 1,000 live births in 1960 to 127 in 1996. In 1980 the U5MR was 227. This represents an average annual reduction rate of 3.6 percent during 1980-96 as compared with a reduction of 1.4 percent between 1960-80. Yet, Bhutan still ranks a lowly thirty-sixth in the world in the U5MR count and needs to further reduce this by nearly fifteen percent by the year 2000. The war against childhood diseases has been stepped up, and as many as ninety-eight percent of the one-year olds are immunised against TB; DPT reaches eighty-seven percent; while immunisation against polio and measles both cover eighty-six percent. The Maternal Mortality Rate nonetheless remains unconscionably high at 1,600 per 100,000 live births, with only fifteen percent of births being attended by trained health workers. Iodine Deficiency Disorders (IDD) have been controlled by mandatory iodisation of salt and by treating thousands of villagers affected by hyperthyroidism. Near universal coverage has been achieved with ninety-six percent of the households in Bhutan now consuming iodised salt.

Education is considered to be the springboard for Bhutan's future development, and the curriculum reflects the aspirations of a modern nation. Between 1990 and 1995, as many as eighty-two percent of primary school children reached grade five. By 2005, the Royal

Multi-cropping is an environmentally sound practice which helps sustain biodiversity while providing good nutrition.

Government hopes to attain universal primary school enrolment, no mean achievement when one remembers that the first batch of twenty students graduated from high school in Bhutan as late as 1968 and that only fifty-nine primary schools existed in the country in 1971. The adult literacy rate is however low with fifty-six percent of males and only twenty-eight percent of females (half the male percentage) being literate. Traditional knowledge and education as well as religious learning are given high priority to ensure that Bhutan's cultural heritage, indigenous medicine and the ancient skills of thankha painting, architecture, handicrafts and music continue to flourish. State-of-the-art technology has been incorporated in education and communication. School textbooks are printed in the country and the *Kuensel* newspaper is a product of desktop publishing. Digital telephone systems link many of the far-flung districts and calling New York now is as simple as dialling Geylegphug. Computers are commonplace in district *dzongs* and schools as they are in business centres in downtown Thimphu.

Education has helped forge a new common ethos, enabling the youth to play an active role in the management of the country. Much of the policy and development planning emanating from Tashichhodzong and from the districts is authored by young professionals. The Bhutanese nurture deep-rooted sentiments for god, king, country and their very own cultural identity. Although many young people have been educated abroad, most return to make use of their expertise within the country and there is little evidence of the brain-drain which afflicts other countries in the region.

Economic and social development in Bhutan has been both a top-down and bottom-up process. Decentralisation has led to a symbiosis within an autonomous framework where community participation and self-help have achieved results with government assistance and foreign aid. The king is devoted to extending the benefits of development to the farthest corners of the kingdom and to ascertain that these are distributed equitably. Environmental safeguards are built into the system to promote conservation of wilderness areas and its unique biodiversity and to ensure that any exploitation of natural resources takes place in a sustainable manner. The king also considers it his historical duty to preserve Bhutan's religious and cultural traditions. While Bhutan is technically not a democracy, this benign exercise of absolute power appears to work well for the common good, and it is refreshing to see the philosophy of development firmly rooted in providing basic needs to all and its fruits actually reaching the people for whom it is meant.

Unlike every other country in South Asia, Bhutan was never colonised—neither by marauding Tibetan warriors nor by the British and it remains a fiercely independent sovereign state. Today, Bhutan pursues a sophisticated foreign policy and has been a member of the United Nations since 1971. It has also been actively involved at other international forums such as the Colombo Plan and the Non-Aligned Movement. As an influential member of the South Asian Association for Regional Cooperation (SAARC) where Bhutan has forged strong ties with neighbouring countries, the king regularly attends summit meetings. An imposing convention hall to accommodate SAARC conferences has been built across the river from Tashichhodzong in Thimphu. Bhutan operates its own airline connecting worldwide destinations through New Delhi, Calcutta, Kathmandu, Dhaka, Yangon and Bangkok, while trade links have been developed with several countries including India, Bangladesh, Thailand and Japan. International development agencies such as the UNDP, FAO, UNICEF, WWF, the World Bank as well as several donor countries have established missions in Thimphu. With Overseas Development Assistance (ODA) inflow in 1995 being US$ 73 million, accounting for as much as twenty-five percent of GNP, Bhutan has maintained a healthy record for project implementation and utilisation of funds, while debt servicing has increased from one percent in 1970 to ten percent in 1995.

Even as telecommunications and the jet age have brought the Dragon Kingdom in close proximity to the rest of the world, Bhutan faces several paradoxes as it prepares to enter the next millennium. Looking beyond its frontiers, the Bhutanese see a world in turmoil. Political opportunism and instability, corruption, communal and ethnic violence, civil strife, lawlessness, and the uprooting of cultural norms in the neighbourhood create a sense of extreme disquiet. Safeguarding the unique cultural identity of Bhutan is therefore not merely a question of faith but of survival itself.

Bhutan has for centuries insulated itself against foreign influences. Its doors were opened to tourism only as late as 1974, but from the very beginning travel was restricted to the privileged few who could afford expensive vacations. Although raking in hard currency was a huge temptation, Bhutan did not want a repeat of the cultural ravaging that took place in Nepal and Ladakh with the opening up of unrestricted tourism. The kingdom has since privatised the tourism industry, but continues to impose strict regulations. Tourists are not permitted to wander about the country at will and monasteries have been kept out of bounds to prevent theft of antiques and valuable artefacts. With the mushrooming of travel agencies, some have tried to remain in business by undercutting rivals with kickbacks and other inducements. So where there was a thin trickle of tourists paying top dollar, there is now an influx of larger numbers but without a corresponding increase in nett earnings.

Increased exposure being a harbinger of change, Bhutan's response has been to enforce cultural norms and codes of conduct which sometimes carry draconian overtones. Ironically, although the monarchy has been regarded as oppressive for implementing these measures, the laws for 'Bhutanisation' were in fact enacted by the National Assembly. Until a few years ago, wearing the traditional dress was mandatory only on formal occasions, at the workplace and when entering a *dzong*. Now western clothes are outlawed in public and the police have the power to enforce the dress code. Younger people, especially, balk at the idea and resort to clever subterfuge to cover up stylish Levi's and designer clothes.

Broadcast television, both terrestrial and satellite, has been banned to prevent the cultural contamination of an impressionable society. The fact is that in the more remote districts of India, including neighbouring Arunachal Pradesh, the advent of the satellite dish has almost overnight wiped out age-old traditions in dress, architecture, social customs, even cuisine, while emulating Bollywood lifestyles. The educated, intellectual elite in Bhutan does not readily buy this argument, pressing instead for access to news, sports and music channels. This is further aggravated by the fact that information and communication highways on the internet are still forbidden despite the availability of computer hardware and fax machines.

The most serious crisis looms on the political front, in what is euphemistically known as the 'International Problem'. Perhaps the least of these problems is the incursion into Bhutanese territory by Bodo (a tribal organisation fighting for autonomy in north-eastern India) and ULFA (United Liberation Front of Asom is an extremist group involved in armed insurgency and extortion) separatists fighting Indian forces in Assam. Many militants take shelter in the Manas Forest, now known in Bhutan as the Namgyel Wangchuk Sanctuary, while others have infiltrated into the southern districts of Samdrup Jonkhar and Geylegphug. Indian authorities have often requested the right of hot pursuit, but Bhutan nervous about finding itself virtually defenceless against the firepower of the terrorists, resisted. Thimphu resisted taking action for many years fearing the firepower of the terrorists. But eventually, in December 2003, the King sent in his army to flush out the militants from the dense forests. Even so, anxiety persists for the potential to foment political instability in the vulnerable and sometimes volatile south.

For years, Bhutan's foothills have been settled by ethnic Nepalese who came in search of greener pastures, their ranks swelled in recent times by migrant workers fleeing the economic hardships of their native land. Although many of Nepalese stock hold positions of influence both in government and in private enterprise, the Royal Government became anxious when a sudden spurt in the minority population became noticeable. The Sikkim example, where the burgeoning Nepalese population had led to the overthrow of the Chogyel, and of the Chinese attempt to deliberately tilt the demographic balance in Tibet, have been the cause of considerable alarm in Thimphu. The ongoing movement for a separate Gorkha homeland in the tea estates of Darjeeling has further exacerbated Bhutan's fears. After 1985,

Philately

Bhutan's extraordinary philately is world-renowned and, since the issue of the first postal stamp in October 1962, a remarkable art form has developed in the kingdom. Stamps have been engraved on steel, screen-printed on silk and etched in gold. Some even play back the national anthem on an audio turntable! Bhutan's stamps displaying thematic coherence and excellent technical quality are considered to be sound investments in international philatelic forums. Reprinted here are some issues reflecting the environmental diversity of Bhutan, particularly of its bird and plant life, and indicate the emphasis laid on conservation of natural habitats and wilderness areas by the Royal Government.

Plant kingdom

Bhutan's ecological regime is a vast gene pool of biodiversity and plant life which makes it an outstanding gallery for the naturalist. Himalayan flowers, plants and medicinal herbs are found in a range of altitudinal zones: in the southern tropical jungles, dipterocarp trees are interspersed with broad-leafed vegetation, tree ferns, palms and bamboo. The middle valleys boast of cherry and apple blossoms, magnolia and wild roses, and over fifty varieties of rhododendron flowers. Colourful amaranths are cultivated in the upper valleys. Pines and conifers blanket mountainsides and the high watersheds. Beyond the tree line, delicate flowers are spread across the Himalayan meadows such as *Gentiana ornata* found near Chomolhari and a bunch of ferns braving the ice and frost in the Phobjika valley.

following the enactment of the Citizenship Act, the Nepalese community in Bhutan was asked to produce evidence, based on records held by the Ministry of Home Affairs, that they or their ancestors had settled in the country before 1958. Subsequent internal strife sent many ethnic Nepalese into exile and thousands have been forced into refugee camps in Nepal. Ironically, many innocent southern Bhutanese have become embroiled in the controversy and have had to face persecution from not just insensitive government functionaries but from vigilante militia which have occasionally conducted a pogrom against so-called 'anti-national elements'. Compounding the ethnic issue is an incipient republican movement which has been gaining momentum threatening to overthrow the Raven Crown of the *Druk Gyalpo*.

His Majesty, preoccupied with matters of state, has forsaken his riverside palace in the vicinity of Tashichhodzong for the seclusion of the woods up in the mountains.

Crown Prince Dasho Jigme Khesar Wangchu attends a public function in Thimphu.

Basketball and archery tournaments have taken a back seat, at least for the present, and the king is not as visible as he used to be in his youth. His four queens, sisters all, live in individual villas in Thimphu, while most of the ceremonial functions have been entrusted to the eighteen-year old Crown Prince, Dasho Jigme Khesar Namgyal Wangchuk, who conducts himself with the same dignity and reserve as his father. On the eve of the next century, Bhutan's future as a monarchy rests on strong foundations and, hopefully, the contentious issues and dissension along the southern borders will soon be amicably settled. Given the Bhutanese penchant for compromise and its egalitarian society, there is no reason why people of different ethnic groups cannot live in harmony within the borders of *Druk Yul*.

Facing page: *The king presides over the inaugural session of the* Tshogdu *in the Great Hall of the National Assembly adorned with exquisite* thankhas.

Chapter 3

Druk Yul

Paro

The Rinpung Dzong – Paro's 'Fortress of Jewels' – commands a sweeping view of the valley. Below the *dzong,* cypress trees line shady paths and weeping willows dip into the Paro Chhu. The river is spanned by a charming wooden bridge covered with a shingled roof. Farm houses clustered together with gaily decorated facades are sheltered by blossoming cherry and peach trees, and terraced paddy fields spread across the valley. Paro is remarkably peaceful, and it is here that Buddhism made its earliest inroads. According to Buddhist tradition, the Tibetan king Songtsen Gampo (AD 629-710) built one hundred and eight temples to subjugate a monstrous demoness who lay across the Himalaya and Tibet. The Jampey Lhakhang in Bumthang was built on the demoness' knee, whereas the Kyiuchu temple in Paro pinned her left foot firmly to the ground.

The Kyiuchu Lhakhang became the lodestone for Buddhist pilgrims and pious mendicants. Guru Rinpoche himself was drawn to Bhutan, visiting the shrine probably in the year 737.

Further upstream on the river, on the way to Drugyel Dzong, Taktsang—the Tiger's Nest—clings precariously to a craggy cliff 800 m (2,600 ft) above the Paro valley. Riding a tigress, Guru Rinpoche is said to have flown to its lair in the mountains and, upon meditating for three months in a cave, assumed the form of *Dorje Droloe,* the Terrifying Thunderbolt. He subjugated the Eight Evil Spirits who hindered the propagation of Buddhism, then proselytized the Paro valley before spreading the Buddha's teachings to the rest of Bhutan.

Taktsang is an intensely spiritual place and contains several significant relics, amongst which are the mortal remains of Langchen Pelkyi Singye, a disciple of Guru Rinpoche, who meditated here around AD 853. Many spiritualists made the pilgrimage to Taktsang in the coming years, but the first sanctuary was built in the fourteenth century by Sonam Gyaltshen, a Tibetan Nyingmapa lama of the Kathogpa sect. An illustration depicting *Zangdopelri,* Guru Rinpoche's mythical paradise, is painted on a rock near the meditation cave. The Kathogpa theologists remained in control until 1645 when Taktsang was handed over to the Shabdrung Ngawang Namgyel and his Nyingmapa master, Rinzing Nyingpo. The Shabdrung expressed a desire to have a temple constructed at the site, but it was left to Tenzing Rabgye, to fulfill his wish at the end of the seventeenth century.

Facing page: The Rinpung dzong, *built by the Shabdrung, dominates Paro valley. Above the fortress is the Ta* dzong, *the watchtower which now houses the National Museum.*
Following pages 46-47: Dance of the Heroes. Pachham *dancers leap in unison in celebration of the victory of good over evil.*

The eclectic fusion of Nyingmapa and Drukpa religious thought emanating from this hallowed eyrie have influenced Bhutan ever since. Having fortified Bhutan against incursions from across the Himalaya and unified the country under Drukpa authority, the Shabdrung masterfully invoked Guru Rinpoche's blessings to legitimise his suzerainty. In 1646, he consecrated the Rinpung Dzong where temples in the central tower are dedicated to lamas of the Drukpa Kagyupa sect as well as to the pantheon of tantric deities. Paintings of both Guru Rinpoche and the Shabdrung adorn the walls. And every year in springtime, a *tsechu* is held at the *dzong* in honour of Guru Padmasambhava.

Perhaps the most spectacular of all *tsechus* in Bhutan, the Paro festival is a highlight in the Bhutanese cultural and tourist calendar. Dances *(chham)*, many of them choreographed by the Shabdrung, celebrate the triumph of Buddhism over its detractors, consecrate the land and bless its people, and disseminate Buddhist ideals through folklore. From the roof of the temple, monks blow on a pair of long horns, and the sound of cymbals, drums and trumpets fill the air. Playing on oboes and trumpets made from the femurs of dead monks, provides good karma to both the musicians and listeners.

On the first day, the proceedings begin within the *dzong*, but are later transferred to the *deyankha*, a courtyard paved with flagstones above the fortress. The dances begin by purifying the venue and protecting it from evil spirits. The Bodhisattva Manjushri, representing the wisdom of all the Buddhas, takes on the aspect of the Lord of Death *(Shinje Choegyel)*. Wearing the wrathful mask of a buffalo, he protects the four directions and blesses them before the appearance of the Gods of Wisdom. The Dance of the Lords of the Cremation Grounds *(Durdag)*, wearing white skull masks and representing skeletons, guard the edges of the *mandala,* the cosmic diagram, where tantric deities reside in eight cremation grounds. These lords neutralise the demonic enemies and show the faithful the way to salvation. In the Dance of the Black Hats *(Shanag)*, the monks beat drums as they slowly and deliberately take possession of the arena by exercising their tantric powers. Their hands take on the shapes of various *mudras* (sacred mystic gestures) and their feet describe mandalas on the ground, according protection and pacifying both inner and outer obstacles. The Shabdrung himself used to perform this very significant tantric ritual dance.

Didactic performances instruct spectators by enacting dramas with moral backgrounds. The Dance of the Judgement of the Dead *(Raksha Manchham)* tells the story of a sinner being sent to hell to the delight of a prancing black demon whereas the virtuous, saved from the demon by the white god, goes to paradise to be welcomed by celestial angels. In judgement stands a large puppet depicting the Lord of Death. The Dance of the Noblemen and Ladies *(Pholey Moley)* tells the story of flirting princesses who are punished for their indiscretions. The Dance of the Stag enacts the tale of a hunter who was converted to Buddhism by the saint Milarepa and gave up hunting.

At the climax of the five-day festival, the courtyard at the *deyankha* fills with people well before dawn despite the freezing cold. A huge *thankha,* or religious painting, is unfurled from the roof of the building. Known as a *thondrel,* it is actually an intricate

Facing page: *Dance of the Judgement of the Dead* (Raksha Marchham). *The Black Demon prances before the Lord of Death, while the White God pleads for forgiveness on behalf of the sinner who has severed a cow's head.*

tapestry of applique work on cloth and is meant to bring salvation to the beholder. The delicate artwork depicts Guru Rinpoche in his eight manifestations along with his two consorts, Mandarava and Yeshey Tshogyel. The devout light butter lamps and place ritual offerings made of dough and butter before the *thondrel*. Dressed in heavy woollen clothes and traditional felt boots, the monks dance cheerfully and, in celebration of the great visual manifestation of the saint, play on a seven-string lute, the *Dranyen*. The giant *thankha* is let down to the ground and ceremoniously rolled and folded away before the first rays of the sun can reach it.

The abbot of Paro Dzong, dressed in full regalia of the Drukpa Kagyupa sect, presides over the *Shugdrel* rituals as the monk body sits in rows receiving alms.

The climax of the Dance of Judgement where the sinner is exonerated and is led in a procession of celestial beings to heaven.

Donning peaked hats and wrapped in dark red habits, the monks ceremoniously beat on double-sided drums with great curved drumsticks. After the *thondrel* has been removed, the eight manifestations of Guru Rinpoche are brought forth with much fanfare in a procession *(Serda Berkhor)*. The principal aspect of the saint, shaded by a large parasol, is paraded around the arena accompanied by a troupe of sixteen fairies, the Goddesses of Offerings. *Pachham* dancers perform the Dance of the Heroes, rattling small double-faced drums *(damaru)* and leap in unison with great acrobatic skill. At the end, the Ging and Tsholing, wearing terrifying masks, recreate scenes of Zangdopelri. Before leaving they exorcise evil and purify the earth. Being tapped on

Facing page: Dranyen Chham. *Monks dance and play the seven-stringed lute before the giant* thondrel *depicting Guru Rinpoche and his consorts.*

the head by the curved drumsticks of the Ging is a blessing which removes impurities from the body.

For five days, the quiet environment of Rinpung Dzong reverberates with the sound and drama of the *tsechu*. A great crush of people, dressed in their finest, throng the courtyard of the *deyankha*, and mill about the many temporary stalls that sell food, drink and trinkets. Mostly, it's a time to eat, drink, flirt and make merry—while adding good spiritual karma!

Above Rinpung Dzong is the Ta Dzong, a watch tower with commanding views of all access routes to the Paro valley. The Ta Dzong now houses the National Museum which represents Bhutanese history as well as works of art and handicrafts. Below the

The sacred thondrel *is lowered to the ground before the first rays of the sun can reach it and is then ceremoniously wrapped by the monks of Paro.*

Ta Dzong, at the confluence of the Dolpo valley and Paro Chhu is the Dungtse Lhakhang which is the only ancient temple in Bhutan in the form of a *chorten*. Built in 1421 by the Tibetan lama, Thangton Gyelpo (1385-1464) on the head of a demoness, the Dungtse Lhakhang is the repository of the finest collection of paintings in Bhutan.

The road along the Paro Chhu climbs gently towards Taktsang and the Drugyel Dzong, beyond which the Snowman's Trek heads into the Greater Himalayan ranges—to Chomolhari, Laya and Lingshi, and on to Lunana. Up the Dolpo valley is the trekking route to Thimphu, and a day's walk gives access to Dakipangtso, an untouched high altitude lake surrounded by mountains and dwarf rhododendron. Spillover from this

Facing page: *Attired in the full regalia of the Drukpa Kagyupa sect, monks don the traditional orange-peaked hats while conducting religious rites.*

saucer-shaped cirque seeps through the forested slopes to mingle eventually with the cascading river Dolpo.

The more convenient route to Thimphu is down the Paro valley to its confluence with the Wang Chhu. Arid and windswept, the lower reaches of the Paro river are a barren wilderness. But the road to Thimphu once again opens into a fertile valley. Namseling is a picturesque village with fruit orchards and terraced farmland, while the mountains above are thick with coniferous forests. At Simtokha, the road veers left to reveal the wide Thimphu basin and one of the most unlikely capital cities of the world.

Thimphu

Phajo Drukgom Shigpo (1184-1251), founder of the Drukpa Kagyupa sect in Bhutan, had a vision that he would find his consort, the reincarnation of a famous *yogini*, in the Wang valley. He first saw the girl of the prophecy, Sonam Pelden, while they stood on either side of the river. Then they both walked along the banks until they met at the only bridge across the river at Lungtenzampa, 'the Bridge of Prophecy'.

For years, the entrance to Thimphu was across a narrow wooden bridge at Lungtenzampa. Festooned with prayer flags and washed with spray from the roaring river, it was a fitting approach to a quaint and charming city. The price of modernisation has seen the construction of a nondescript concrete structure which could belong to any other city, but not to Thimphu. Prayer flags do not grace this bridge because they do not belong to this alien piece of architecture, and even the sound of the river is absorbed by the concrete.

The Thimphu valley is at an elevation of 2,350 m (7,700 ft). Urbanisation began here when Thimphu was proclaimed to be the national capital in 1952 and the Dechenchoeling Palace was built at this time. Even today, the city retains its ethnic architectural style. Although many new constructions incorporate only the facade of Bhutanese style windows to conform with government regulations, many houses are still built in the traditional way. Following a real-estate boom, Thimphu of the 'nineties has witnessed a somewhat haphazard urban development, the major culprit being overcrowded and unimaginative multi-storied government housing and tenements. As with many other Asian markets, a large number of inexpensive, reconditioned cars have been imported from Japan where these vehicles are not street-legal for want of requisite emission control equipment. As a result, for the first time ever, Thimphu faces signs of atmospheric pollution.

Yet, unlike other capital cities in the world, Thimphu remains essentially pastoral in character and changes its demeanour with the seasons. Agricultural terraces are farmed in the fertile valley, fruit orchards line the gentler slopes while the high mountains are blanketed by coniferous forests. The imposing Tashichhodzong looks onto farmlands and a golf course. A riot of colour envelops the *dzong* as wild cosmos bloom through summer into late autumn. In springtime, cherry blossoms light up the well-manicured palace lawns.

Facing page: Monks perform the dance of the Ging and Tsholing at Tashichhodzong.
Following pages 56-57: Tashichhodzong besieged by a rage of wildflowers as monsoon clouds gather overhead.

The Tashichhodzong, which houses the Royal Secretariat as well as the chambers of the Je Khenpo, is located in a picturesque setting by the banks of the river. But it is clearly not intended to be a bulwark of defence, unlike the other fortresses built in Bhutan by the Shabdrung Ngawang Namgyel. The original *dzong* in Thimphu was located at Dechen Phodrang which is now a monastic school. The Do Ngon Dzong, 'Fortress of the Blue Stone', was strategically placed on a high promontory and had a chequered history. The Shabdrung took control of the *dzong* in the 1630s and rebuilt it. Calling the *dzong* by its present name, Tashichhodzong, he made it the summer residence of the monk body. The Tashichhodzong was established at its present location in the latter part of the eighteenth century by the Je Khenpo but was

Nordzin Lam, main street in downtown Thimphu. A policeman directs traffic at one of the two manned intersections in the capital.

reconstructed by the late king, H.M. Jigme Dorji Wangchuk in the 1960s as the seat of government under the new dispensation. Exquisite collections of religious *thankhas* adorn the walls of the Royal Secretariat and the old Hall of the National Assembly where the king sits on a gilded throne.

A favourite pastime on weekends is to attend a game of archery at the Changlimithang grounds where contestants use both traditional bows made of bamboo as well as the more sophisticated spring bows. Triumphant war whoops accompany a strike, while the opposing team dances around the metre-high wooden target calling upon the spirits to shake the archer's aim. Food and drink accompanied by somewhat ribald humour make it a pleasant way to spend an afternoon. Changlimithang is the battleground where the Tongsa Penlop, Ugyen Wangchuk won a decisive victory in 1885 to wrest firm control of the country before assuming the crown as the first king of Bhutan. The battle was a turning point in the history of Bhutan marking the end of internal strife which had torn the country apart since the late seventeenth century.

Every weekend, a bazaar is held by the riverside near Changlimithang where villagers bring their wares from distant farms and hamlets. Fresh vegetables, young ferns, chillies, balls of cottage cheese, red potatoes, *doma* and betel leaf, mushrooms and eggs, slivers of dried fish and meat are spread out in little stalls. Tibetan trinkets, silverware, stones, *bangchus* and bows and arrows, even the latest issue of *Kuensel*, the weekly newspaper, can be found here. Shopping at the bazaar and mingling with friends, followed by a breakfast of pork fat and Bhutanese salted tea or *chhang* if your

Low clouds hang over Thimphu which retains its pastoral character despite recent urbanisation.

preference is for something more stimulating, makes for an interesting start to a Saturday morning.

Above Changlimithang is the city centre, dominated by a clock tower and built alongside roads at two levels. This is where all the shopping is. Book stores, travel agents, curio shops, general merchants as well as hotels and banks. The government emporium is a convenient outlet for a variety of textiles, handicrafts and objets d'art. For the philatelist, the Central Post Office is an essential stopover to pick up a collection of exquisite stamps.

The traditional rendezvous in Thimphu is the Swiss Bakery, a circular chalet with large glazed windows which serves tea and coffee with muffins, pastry and patties in a warm atmosphere. The maitre d'hotel is Tourie, a Swiss man who prefers to go by his Bhutanese name, Tsering and keeps up his penchant for gadgets. The bakery

comes fitted with an electronic weather station, solar power and a clever locking system for the toilet door! The Plums Cafe across the road serves sumptuous meals with a good view of the city centre and the surrounding mountains. Further down the hill is the favourite watering hole in Thimphu, the Sambhara Pub, frequented by the smart younger set of Thimphu. It keeps a good bar, serves succulent spare ribs and generates warmth and bonhomie. Kash, the owner, is a keen fisherman and more than willing to share his catch of rainbow trout with the clientele—counted more as his friends than his customers. On Saturday nights, a dark downtown alley livens up to a swinging but makeshift discotheque frequented by the young and upwardly mobile.

The Swiss Bakery, a favourite rendezvous in the heart of the town.

A prominent landmark in Thimphu is the Memorial Chorten built as a tribute to the late king, H.M. Jigme Dorji Wangchuk. Along with the Dungtse Lhakhang in Paro, this is the only temple in Bhutan which is shaped like a *chorten*. At the foot of the valley is the Simtokha Dzong, the first fortress consecrated by the Shabdrung Ngawang Namgyel in 1631. It is now a centre for Dzongkhag studies.

The Motithang district, the 'Meadow of Pearls', is the upmarket residential area of Thimphu. Up in the woods is the old Motithang Hotel which was built in 1974 for the coronation of H.M. Jigme Singye Wangchuk. State guests, royalty and other celebrities have all been enchanted by the elegance and grace the hotel offered, but today it lies forlorn and unsure of its future. Perhaps one day it will be restored to its old glory.

Facing page: *Fresh vegetables bring colour to the weekend bazaar.*

Motithang is the staging ground for the trek to Phajoding and the monastery at 3,700 m (12,200 ft) where the saint Phajo Drukgom Shigpo meditated in the thirteenth century. Above the monastery is a log cabin with a large glazed verandah which provides a panoramic view of Thimphu, especially at night. Across the 4,100 m (13,500 ft) ridge, the path leads to the Jimilangtso lakes where trout may be found, but the intense cold and icy fog should keep any but the most desperate angler at bay.

From Tashichhodzong, the road winds its way along the left bank of the Thinchhu to the Dechenchoeling Palace, residence of H.M. the Queen Mother Ashi Kesang. The road continues up the valley to the entrance of the Jigme Dorji National Park from where a mule track leads into the higher mountains to eventually join the Snowman's

Convivial watering hole at the Sambhara pub.

Trek to Chomolhari, Laya, Lingshi and Lunana. It is also possible to walk from Dechenchoeling through farmland and villages up to the woods where the monasteries of Tango and Cheri nestle.

The Tango Monastery was built in the thirteenth century by Phajo Drukgom Shigpo and inherited by his son Dampa, ancestor of the Drukpa nobility of Paro. The Shabdrung Ngawang Namgyel was hosted here upon his arrival in Bhutan by Tsewang Tenzin, a reincarnation of the Phajo and grandson of Drukpa Kunley, the Divine Madman, who remains a popular figure in Bhutan for his somewhat unorthodox and often crude methods of preaching. The Shabdrung found a wife for Tsewang Tenzin, and their son, Tenzin Rabgye, was born in 1638. A protege of the

Facing page: *Monks walk along a quiet path below Tango monastery where the former Je Khenpo now resides in retirement.*

Shabdrung, he became the fourth Desi, last in the lineage of the Gya clan. Ousted from Thimphu in 1694 by the forces of Gedun Choephel, the Punakha Dzongpoen, Tenzin Rabgye retired to Tango and ended his days there. This brought to an end a tradition of succession observed for fifteen generations and threw Bhutan into turmoil for the next two centuries, until the present dynasty came to power and restored order.

Across the river from Tango, a traditional wooden bridge cantilevered on stones on either bank, leads the way to Cheri Monastery, built by the Shabdrung in 1620 as his residence. Nowadays, the sixty-seventh Je Khenpo, Trulku Ngawang Thinley Lhundrup, lives in retirement here.

Facing page & above: Dance of the Terrifying Deities (Tungam). *The gods encircle evil spirits before ritualistically slaying them.*

Punakha

The Dochu La watershed at 3,116 m (10,200 ft) separates the Thimphu valley from Punakha. Himalayan blue magpies glide from magnolia trees to rhododendrons extending their long tails and showing off their brilliant plumage. In winter, fir trees droop under a heavy blanket of snow, and icicles hang from frozen waterfalls. On a clear day, Dochu La offers a stunning view of the snow-capped Himalayan ranges including the summits of Masangang and Jejekangphugang, both standing at 7,158 m (23,480 ft), and Gangkar Punsum (25,000 ft). A log cabin offers tea and biscuits and a

Following pages 66-67: The Je Khenpo, His Holiness Trulku Jigme Choedar, watches as monks perform ritual dances at the Punakha Dromche.

powerful pair of binoculars for a closer look at the mountains. Traffic over the pass moves clockwise around a *chorten* and passes under colourful prayer flags stretched across the highway, before beginning the long descent into Punakha which nestles in a river valley at an elevation of about 1,700 m (5,500 ft). The road passes through a variety of ecosystems with the fir trees of Dochu La giving way to temperate pine and oak forests and then to sub-tropical vegetation of giant ferns, orchids and banana plantations. Some of the most attractive villages in Bhutan lie on the way to Lobeysa where the road bifurcates for Punakha.

The Punakha Dzong was built in 1637 by the Shabdrung Ngawang Namgyel adjacent to a temple which had been established as far back as 1328 by the saint

The Punakha dzong *at the confluence of the Mo Chhu and Po Chhu.*

Ngagi Rinchen. The fortress remained under the tutelage of the Dzongpoens until it became the capital of Bhutan. The first king, H.M. Ugyen Wangchuk's reign was inaugurated here in the Palace of Great Bliss on 17 December 1907, the Year of the Fire-Sheep. The coronation was attended by a British mission under John Claude White, a personal friend of the king, along with other officers and twenty-five men from the Punjab Regiment. In January 1910, the Treaty of Punakha cemented Bhutan's ties with the British Raj in India. Jigme Wangchuk, the second king, was also crowned at Punakha in March 1927 and it remained the seat of government until 1952 when the third king, H.M. Jigme Dorji Wangchuk, decided to transfer his capital to Thimphu.

Facing page: *Amidst much fanfare, Pazap warriors rush down the steep steps of Punakha* dzong *to re-enact the fierce battles waged against Tibetan invaders.*

The Punakha Dzong drives a great wedge between the Mo Chhu and Po Chhu. Flocks of brahmany ducks and long-necked cormorants skim over the waters in a tight formation. A variety of crops are cultivated on the fertile banks of the rivers and it is not uncommon to have different grains ripening for harvest on the same field, an eco-friendly system that has held good for generations. A lot of land and livestock in Punakha is owned by the wealthier inhabitants of Thimphu who prefer to spend the winter in the warmer climate of the lower valleys. The Shabdrung himself established the tradition by making Punakha his winter capital and even now, the monk body migrates to Punakha to escape the harsher weather of Thimphu. In 1651, the Shabdrung entered retreat at the *dzong* from which he never reappeared. Incredibly, his death

Snow covers the pass at Dochu La.

was kept secret for fifty long years to enable the Drukpas to maintain their tenuous hold over the region.

The great flood of 1994 brought mayhem to the environs of the *dzong*. The Dzongchun (Little *Dzong*), the original temple, has been rebuilt, and the entire citadel has been given a facelift. New revetments and levees have changed the course of the river and strengthened flood protection measures, but the alterations have changed the original picturesque setting where the rivers almost lapped at the walls of the *dzong*.

In earlier times, havoc was wrought by the marauding Tibetan armies who rode into the valley across the mountain passes from Laya and Gasa in order to retrieve a

Facing page: *Monks congregate outside the monastery at Punakha, the winter residence of the Je Khenpo.*

sacred relic. The bone of contention was a statue of Avalokiteshvara, the Ranjung Karsapani, said to be a vertebra of Tsangpa Gyare, founder of the Drukpa school in Tibet, which was discovered among his mortal remains during his cremation. The Punakha *dzong* proved to be an effective bulwark of defence, and the Bhutanese forces were able to repulse repeated attacks.

Every year at the end of winter in the first month of the lunar year, a *Dromche* takes place at the Punakha Dzong. The village of Punakha comes alive during the festival with restaurants and stalls doing brisk business as people from as far away as Laya, distinguished by their conical hats made of cane, come to the valley.

The monks in residence at the *dzong* spend hours chanting Buddhist mantras in deep, bass tones producing sounds like an orchestra of string instruments interspersed occasionally with trumpets, drums and cymbals. The festival, dedicated to Yeshe Gompo, a manifestation of Mahakala, the protective deity of Bhutan, is presided over by the Je Khenpo himself. The abbot, dressed in customary yellow, sits on a balcony overlooking a wide courtyard where the religious dances are performed.

Re-enacting the drama of the Tibetan incursions, troops in red uniforms rush out of the *dzong*, flourishing swords at the head of steep wooden stairs at the entrance. With the deafening sound of firecrackers, the *Pazaps* leap onto horsebacks to ride into battle. The troops are camped in four different locations around the *dzong*, where ritual dances are performed to seek the protection of the deities while the warriors fortify themselves with alcohol. The *Serda Berkhor* procession at the end of the festivities is led by the Je Khenpo who comes out of the *dzong* amidst great fanfare, led by troops and *Pachham* dancers, to pray on the banks of the river and to proclaim the victory of the Bhutanese forces.

Wangdi Phodrang

Wangdi Phodrang lies at the confluence of two rivers. A long mountain spur extends into the drainage system of the Dang Chhu as it flows down from the north while the Mo Chhu, meandering its way from Punakha, gently flows along the southern length of the spur in the shadow of the *dzong*. Terraced fields lead down to the riverbed which is lined in places by white, sandy beaches. Wangdi Phodrang is nicknamed 'Windy' Phodrang because of the high velocity wind which gusts over the hills, particularly in the afternoon. Shelter belts of trees have been raised but the gale, raising swirls of dust, blows right through, permanently bending the tall-stands of eucalyptus.

The Wangdi Phodrang *dzong* was built in the mid-seventeenth century under directions given by the Shabdrung Ngawang Namgyel and completed in 1683 by Tenzing Rabgye. Its roof of shingles is held down in the traditional manner by heavy stones. Two large prayer wheels greet the visitor on either side of the entrance which opens onto a courtyard surrounded by buildings. On the far end is the main temple building from which, on the climax of the annual festival in September, a large *thondrel* depicting Guru Rinpoche is unfurled at dawn. Ritual offerings of butter lamps cast an eerie light while *Pachcham* dancers, dwarfed by the huge tapestry, beat small double-

Facing page: A giant thondrel *depicting Guru Padmasambhava is unfurled at dawn during the Wangdi Phodrang tsechu.*

Following pages 74-75: The abbot of Wangdi Phodrang presides over ritual prayers. The monks *wear peaked orange hats of the Drukpa Kagyupa tradition.*

sided drums *(damaru)* in celebration. Drukpa Kagyupa traditions are very evident here with the monks attired in ceremonial orange hats and regalia.

Across the river from Wangdi, saddled in an arid gully, is the village of Rinchengang. Its houses look remarkably nondescript and the earth-colours exaggerate their monotony. Ironically, the village is renowned for its masons. Age-old traditions of stone-cutting and construction of *dzongs* emanate from this village and the master craftsmen of Rinchengang have been responsible even in recent times for the rebuilding of the Punakhadzong and the Tashichhodzong. Their skills are also harnessed for the construction of houses, temples, *chortens* and bridges built in the indigenous style.

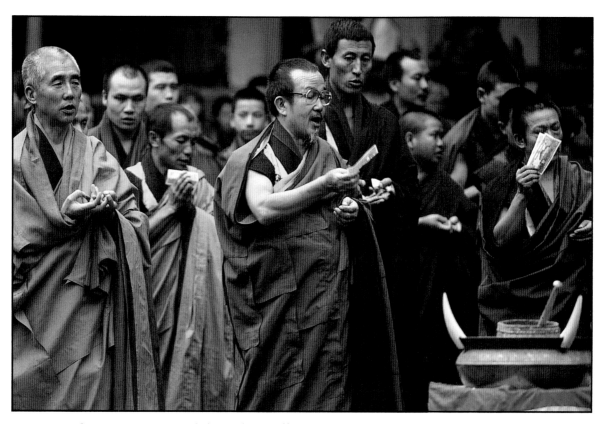

Monks recite prayers while making offerings at an altar decorated with yak horns.

Wangdi—the place where the Shabdrung had foreseen that a flock of ravens may fly off in four directions—lies at the crossroads of Bhutan. A new route follows the river south to Chirang while the east-west central highway cuts across the country through this little township. Following the valley of the Dang river, the road winds its way across the watershed of the Black Mountains at the 3,390 m (11,200 ft) Pele La pass. A few miles short of Pele La, an unpaved trail branches off near Nobding village to Gantey and the Phobjika valley.

Engaging a four-wheel drive, the hardy off-roader bumps and slides its way through oak and rhododendron forests to Phobjika, a wide glacial basin still marshy from melting ice and snow. These are the winter nesting grounds of the rare and endangered

Facing page: *Wearing* ghos *and white* kamne, *men accompany women dressed in* kiras, *to the* dzong.

black-necked cranes *(Grus nigricollis)*. After their marathon flight across the mountains from Central Asia, the cranes seem to celebrate by trumpeting loudly and displaying a spectacular dance routine. Flocks of the long-limbed birds take off in a gentle climb, their wings working hard to gather lift, then spread out to glide elegantly along the high mountain ridges.

Gantey Gompa is set on a hill overlooking the Phobjika valley. The monastery was built in 1613 by Pema Trinley, grandson of the Nyingmapa saint, Pema Lingpa. This is the largest Nyingmapa monastery in Bhutan, and the only one west of the Black Mountains. The Gantey Trulkus (reincarnations of Pema Trinley) maintained harmonious relations with the dominant Drukpas yet continued to propagate the religious traditions

Black-necked cranes (Grus nigricollis) *wintering at Phobjika soar majestically above the valley.*

taught by Pema Lingpa. The second Trulku, Tenzing Legpe Dondrup (1645-1726) extended the monastery and built a *dzong* around it.

Phobjika village is a cluster of traditional houses. A couple of sprawling homes on the far end of the valley are particularly spacious and comfortable and take in travellers as guests. There is no electricity here, which adds to the charm of living in a traditional Bhutanese village home. Steep stairways cut into tree trunks lead into the dark hallways of the lower floors. The upper floors are well-lit and airy, and a wood-fired stove brings heat to the living quarters. These homes are the realms of silence, with all the inhabitants quietly going about their chores.

A day's walk from Phobjika leads to Khaybithang where a Nature Study Centre has been established. A permanent exhibition was mounted here at its inauguration during the National Day celebrations in December 1996. This area is the habitat of different species of birds and wildlife, and herds of wild yak graze on their favourite diet of high-altitude dwarf bamboo.

Crossing the Black Mountain at Pele La is significant. This was the frontier of the Tongsa Penlop with his western neighbours, and this is the divide which the 'mad saint' Drukpa Kunley (1455-1529) had refused to cross. He is said to have scattered mustard seeds across the eastern valleys and ever since rice could not be cultivated. The land of the 'Black Mountain Bjop' is a gently undulating grassland with scattered mustard fields in sharp contrast to the terraced paddy fields and thickly forested western flank of the mountains. The Bjopas raise sheep and yak and fashion wicker baskets and *bangchus* from the abundantly available dwarf bamboo.

Gantey gompa, *a sanctuary of the Nyingmapa sect, overlooks the Phobjika valley.*

Eleven kilometres east of Pele La is the village of Rukubji where the houses are built at the lower edge of a cultivated tableland. The plateau sloping down between the two mountains is considered to be a serpent, and the location of the temple on its head signifies the subjugation of its harmful aspects by the good spirit of Buddhism. Guru Rinpoche himself is credited with having vanquished the snake demoness and exorcised the land of its evil spirits. The advent of the national highway brought in its wake much mayhem, and the inhabitants of Rukubji felt that the rising dust, the sound of dynamite blasting to clear rocks, and ensuing traffic on the road would awaken the sleeping demoness. Advice from the local priest to move the resident deity to another spot added to the confusion, and the sense of upheaval was enhanced with a series of inauspicious incidents, amongst them a poor harvest and the deaths of some villagers. Eventually, the Gantey Trulku was asked to mediate and restore order by reinstating the deity in its original place.

Tongsa

Along the road to Tongsa is the Chendebji *chorten*, its stylised eyes peering out over a row of *mani* stones. Built in the mid-eighteenth century by Lama Sida to pin down a demoness who threatened the valleys, the *chorten* is modelled on the lines of the Nepalese *stupas* of Bodhnath and Swayambhunath. In 1982, the Queen Mother Ashi Kesang had a Bhutanese style *chorten* built in the vicinity.

Tongsa comes into view long before reaching it. The old path descends into the gorge and rises steeply up to the *dzong*. But the motorable road follows the contours of the mountains and takes a circuitous route into an adjacent valley before arriving at

Tongsa dzong *with its V-shaped watchtower, the Ta* dzong, *maintains a strategic position at Bhutan's crossroads.*

Tongsa. It's perplexing because one can imagine a bridge connecting the road to the *dzong*, yet it takes the better part of an hour to cover the twenty kilometres to reach it. Viewing the *dzong* from so many different angles, however, lends a perspective on the strategic importance of the *dzong* which eventually placed its Penlop at the helm of a unified country when Ugyen Wangchuk became the first king of Bhutan. To this day, the Crown Prince of Bhutan is appointed Penlop of Tongsa, signifying its historical importance.

In the seventeenth century, Bhutan was split into three major spheres of political influence shared between the Penlops of Tongsa, Paro and Dagana. Eventually, Paro

Facing page: *Various ethnic groups mingle in Bhutan. These wizened features possibly trace Tibetan lineage.*

gained control of western Bhutan, while Tongsa exerted its hegemony over the central and eastern regions. Following the Duar War in 1864 and the Treaty of Sinchula by which Bhutan ceded the Duars to the British in return for an annuity, the Penlop of Tongsa, Jigme Namgyel, asserted his authority over Bhutan. His son, Ugyen Wangchuk, succeeded to the governorship in 1881 and in 1885, inflicted a crushing defeat on his opponents in Thimphu. He strengthened relations with the British and was awarded with a knighthood for his efforts.

The Tongsa Dzong at an elevation of 2,200 m (7,200 ft) has a commanding view of the Mangde valley. A sharp vigilance was maintained over the defences of Tongsa from the V-shaped watch-tower of the Ta Dzong. The first *chorten* was built here by Ngagi

The Chendebji chorten *sets its gaze across the valley.*

Wangchuk (1517-54), the great-grandfather of Shabdrung Ngawang Namgyel. Recognising the strategic advantages of Tongsa, the Shabdrung constructed the first *dzong* at this site, after which it witnessed several expansions and repairs. The location of the original 'Temple of Chortens' also includes the *chorten* of Ngagi Wangchuk.

Tongsa lies at the junction of east and west as well as the far south. The southern route leads to Shemgang, an area wrapped in tropical forests. Bananas, mangoes, ferns, lichen, bamboos and orchids thrive here. Geylegphug cradles the foothills where river valleys open onto the plains and, in the extreme south, the Manas forest teems with wildlife. Geologists have unearthed ores of copper and lignite near Gonkhola and the Black Mountains too are reputed to be rich in minerals. The road to the east climbs up to the Yutong La at 3,400 m (11,200 ft) providing views of the 25,000 ft Gangkar Punsum, Bhutan's highest summit. It's once again yak country up here with plenty of bamboo. Beyond the pass, deep coniferous forests reach into the Chumey valley of Bumthang.

Bumthang

A place like Bumthang lends itself to ghost stories. It's an enchanted land filled with myth and legend, where people with deep faith and belief tell tales of marauding warriors and proselytizing monks, where homes are painted with religious symbols and people wear charms to keep evil at bay. The Choekhor valley is dominated by the imposing Jakar Dzong dating back to the sixteenth century. At night, fog rises from the river and mysterious fires light up marshy bogs.

Early one wintry morning, a film crew was preparing for the day's shoot, cleaning lenses, checking batteries and getting reluctant jeep engines to start in the cold. Robert Tyabji, the director, was collecting his thoughts when an old man ambled past the guest house and continued along a narrow path down to the river. More to shake off the cold than out of any curiosity, Robert followed the old man to the river but was galvanised into action when he saw him casually step into the water and vanish from sight. Thinking he had drowned, Robert ran back to the guest house to seek help for a rescue, but was told by the caretaker that the old man was a ghost who lived in a whirlpool in the river and that his appearance could well be ominous. That same afternoon, a boating accident tragically took the lives of two Swiss doctors who had been living and working in Bumthang.

Bumthang is Bhutan's spiritual cradle. The name itself carries religious connotations, meaning literally 'a plain shaped like a *bumpa*', an oblong-shaped lustral water vase used in religious rituals. Guru Padmasambhava, Bhutan's patron saint, introduced Buddhism to Bumthang in the eighth century, and is said to have meditated at the site of the Kurje Lhakhang. The revered saints, Longchen Rabjampa and Dorje Lingpa preached here in the fourteenth century and Pema Lingpa (1450-1521), one of the greatest religious masters of Bhutan, established the Tamshing Lhakhang which, to this day, has remained the fountainhead of Nyingmapa traditions. The Jampey Lhakhang, built in the seventh century by the Tibetan king Songtsen Gampo, even predates the arrival of Guru Rinpoche.

The dominant Drukpa Kagyupa influence was relatively late in coming, and Bumthang capitulated politically only in the seventeenth century when Bhutan was first unified by the Shabdrung Ngawang Namgyel. Bumthang was ruled since very early times by offshoots of Tibetan royalty, whereas in western Bhutan a Drukpa religious nobility held the reins of power. The Bhutanese royal family, which traces its ancestry to both Nyingmapa and Drukpa forebears, also has strong affiliations with Bumthang. The first king of Bhutan, Ugyen Wangchuk, was born here at the Wangduchoeling Palace of the Tongsa Penlop, Jigme Namgyel. He built a temple at Kurje to commemorate the site where Guru Rinpoche's body was imprinted on a rock. One of the most sacred places in Bhutan, the Kurje monastery was the site chosen to conduct the last rites for H.M. Jigme Dorji. A temple was built here by the Queen Mother, H.M. Ashi Kesang Wangchuk, enclosing the entire complex into a three-dimensional *mandala*. A hundred and eight stone stupas stand vigil at the spot and a litany of prayer flags, fluttering incessantly in the breeze, send forth the message of the Buddha.

Four river valleys unite in the Bumthang basin. The Chumey and Choekhor valleys, at somewhat lower altitudes, are conducive for agriculture. Buckwheat is the staple here, but wheat and barley are also grown. The Tang and Ura valleys are higher and colder and better suited for rearing sheep, although the introduction of potato farming

has brought a degree of prosperity to the region. Above all, the Chumey valley is reputed for its weavers who work pedal looms to produce woollen cloth with exquisite designs known as *yatha*. Zugney village is particularly well-known and presents a feast for the eyes as a number of young women weave intricate patterns against the backdrop of an array of *yatha* pieces.

The Chumey valley has several old monasteries dating back to the founders of the Nyingmapa school. Tharpaling monastery at 3,600 m (11,900 ft) was established by Longchen Rabjampa in the fourteenth century. Near the weavers' village of Zugney is Pra Lhakhang built in the sixteenth century by Tenpe Nyima, grandson of Pema Lingpa. A short walk from Prakhang, secluded in a forest, is the century-

Wangdichoeling Palace, birthplace of the first king of Bhutan, with Jakar dzong, Monastery of the White Bird, dominating the Choekhor valley.

old Nyimalung monastery which houses about a hundred monks.

Perched above the Choekhor valley is Jakar Dzong, 'Monastery of the White Bird', built in the sixteenth century by the Drukpa lama, Ngagi Wangchuk, great-grandfather of the Shabdrung Ngawang Namgyel. This is the only *dzong* in Bhutan which does not house a Drukpa monastic community although it is the administrative seat of the district. The town of Jakar is little more than a village with some shops and wayside restaurants. A road leads up to the Wangduchoeling Palace, then onto the Jampey Lhakhang and Kurje monasteries. Across the river from Kurje is the Tamshing monastery which has some of the oldest murals and paintings in Bhutan. It is also home to a

Facing page: *Painstaking work is required to weave intricate designs on traditional handlooms. Window light illuminates a* yatha *weaver in Ura.*

small monastic community and the teachings of Pema Lingpa are imparted to young monks or *geylongs*.

Jampey Lhakhang may not be as visually spectacular as some of the other monasteries in the region, perhaps because of its vintage. Indeed, here lies its enduring charm. Thirteen centuries old and still maintaining its ancient traditions, it is reputed to have been built on the knee of a demoness to pin her down; the rest of this Satan extended all the way into Tibet. The Jampey Lhakhang festival or *drup*, is held each year around November and carries on for five days. Many of the rituals and dances hark back to the days of the Nyingmapa masters, extolling the virtues of Guru Rinpoche, the triumph of good over evil, and climaxes in a ceremony to bless the spectators.

Once a poor shepherd's village, Ura now exudes a sense of prosperity.

The festival begins late in the evening with the Dance of the Black Hats and the Ging. Monks dancing in full regalia perform a purification ceremony, consecrating the earth with alcohol and grain. Fires are lit to exorcise evil and, in the darkness, the fearsome visage of masked dancers is accentuated in the flickering light of fires and flares. The Dance of the Naked Lama harks back to ancient tantric rituals, but this is performed late at night and zealously shielded from foreign eyes. In the Dance of the Ging and Tsholing, incarnations of Guru Rinpoche bring blessings and remove obstacles to the doctrine of the Buddha. There are Dances from Paradise (*Dramitse Ngacham*) and the Dance of the Heroes (*Pachham*) taught to the monks by Pema Lingpa.

Atsaras, the clowns wearing funny red masks, keep the spectators entertained. Slapstick humour is a part of their routine at every *tsechu* or *dromche*, and even tourists do not escape their attention. But there is also a serious side to their antics. The harvest season is the time for fertility rites and the *atsaras* get into the act of anointing young women with wooden phalluses from which a milky fluid pours in a thin trickle from a strategically placed orifice!

Jampey is very much a village festival. In the open courtyard of the monastery, against the backdrop of forested mountains dusted with a light covering of snow, villagers from every valley in Bumthang gather to participate in the *drup*. Slivers of smoked yak, chilli pork and buckwheat pancakes emerge from cane *bangchus* as families picnic while watching masked dancers swirl about to the sound of cymbals, drums and horns. Being at the Jampey Drup is a pleasant experience without having to contend with jostling crowds and the crush of foreign tourists,

Against the colourful backdrop of yatha, *weavers work at their looms in Zugney village in the Chumey valley.*

unlike many of the other festivals which are held in the grandeur of the big *dzongs*. At the end of the five-day festival, the resident deity is brought out in a ceremonial procession and blessings are showered upon all gathered at this auspicious moment.

In the late seventies and early eighties, a number of Swiss families settled in Bumthang. Even without electricity and other modern conveniences, the expatriate community made itself quite comfortable experimenting with innovative technology. Solar and wind energy were harnessed and convective systems used for heating. The table had a selection of home-made salami, bread from the oven, jam from handpicked strawberries and apples, pots of wild honey, and tea flavoured with nutmeg and cinnamon. A Swiss guest-house with the feel of an Himalayan chalet and set in orchards of fruit trees, still exists and continues with these traditions.

The locals also learnt the art of producing cheese, cider, apple juice and honey and Bumthang has now become renowned for these products.

East from Choekhor, is the Tang valley. The river cuts through a narrow gorge and opens out onto Mebartso—Flaming Lake—one of the most sacred pilgrimage sites in Bhutan. The devout float lamps on the water and bring the ashes of the dead to this spot where Pema Lingpa is said to have found religious treasures hidden by Guru Rinpoche. Mebartso is in fact not a lake. The river swirls in eddies before rushing on down the chasm, while moisture from the spray ensures lush foliage and the genesis of a variety of rare plants.

Ura La is a pass at 3,600 m (11,900 ft) which opens onto the Ura valley. High

Pachham *dancers leap into the air at Jampey Lhakhang, one of the oldest monasteries in Bhutan which adheres to the Nyingmapa tradition.*

altitude pastures support sheep farms and winter grazing for yak. The village of Ura at an altitude of 3,000 m (10,000 ft) has an architectural style of its own. The houses are made of grey stone with shingle roofs and clustered close together. Before potato farming brought prosperity and a school building, Ura was decidedly a poorer community. Nowadays, the houses appear to be well maintained and the children are educated with a positive outlook on the future. Ura village indeed epitomises the process of development and modernisation in Bhutan. Basic needs have been directed at the poorest communities and development has made a tangible difference to the lives of common people in a relatively short time.

Facing page: *An* atsara *anoints young maidens with a wooden phallus during the Drup festival at Jampey Lhakhang.*

Chapter 4

Chomolhari: Abode of the Goddess

A light drizzle hangs in a melancholic haze over the ramparts of the Drugyel Dzong, its crumbling stone walls consumed by fire and the ravages of time over the past 350 years. Built by Shabdrung Ngawang Namgyel in 1647 following his triumphant march over the Tibetans, the fortress looms forbiddingly over a rocky outcrop, a strategic sentinel guarding the Paro valley from further incursion. The ridge is indeed a geographical divide that separates the verdant, fertile fields of Paro from the cold, windswept rocky terrain which ascends into the snowbound Himalayan mountains and beyond to the high Tibetan plateau.

The road from Paro terminates here at this junction of two worlds. This is the physical frontier which separates wilderness from modern civilisation and the internal combustion engine. From here on, grit, stamina and inventiveness hold sway, and real power comes not from electricity but from draught animals: bullocks to plough fields, mules to carry loads and horses to ride on. In the higher reaches, no other animal will manage except the wild, ill-tempered and unpredictable yak. At the foot of the *dzong*, mules impatiently stamp their hooves against the cold, waiting to be loaded with sacks of pots and pans, camping gear and a variety of food ranging from rice and potatoes to eggs, cheese, pork and poultry. The village is brimming with excitement at this early hour, preparing for the mule trains to begin the long journey up the mountains. It's time to collect my personal pack and move on, leaving the squabbling muleteers to sort out their affairs and join me later.

The swirling mists wrapped around Drugyel begin to lift as brilliant sunshine bursts through the drifting clouds to unveil a sharp blue sky. Against this backdrop, towering above the ruins, emerges the sparkling white summit of Chomolhari, which the Bhutanese revere as the Goddess. The sight of the sacred mountain is a good omen, but it's a long walk to get there—three or four days under the best conditions—and I can only hope for fair weather along the way. By the month of November it's somewhat late in the season to hike in the Himalaya, but the morning nip adds a charge of well-being as I set off into the mountains, savouring the heady feeling that almost always accompanies the start of an expedition.

This is harvest time at these elevations; lower down, in the environs of Paro, it will be a few weeks yet before the paddy ripens. A flurry of glistening chaff wafts across terraced fields as women winnow the grain in wicker trays and men paddle thresh mills. The red rice grown here is prized for the flavour it imparts to Bhutanese cuisine. I've made sure my rations include the Paro red rice with plenty of chillies, pork, vermicelli noodles, and *datsi*—the local cottage cheese which is best a little rancid when it exudes its characteristic odours.

I traverse a narrow suspension bridge, which bounces and swings with every

Facing page: *The Chomolhari summit rises above the cascading Paro river near Takthangka.*

step, to cross over to the left bank of the raging Pachu. Reflecting the warm colours of autumn but icy cold from melting glaciers, the river will be my constant companion as I hike up the valley. This watershed is an environmental paradise, stretching from the thick vegetation of the foothills to the evergreen temperate forests of silver oak and blue pine. Himalayan firs and rhododendrons blanket the high ridges and, beyond the tree line, Himalayan meadows nurture the most fragile flowering plants despite the intense cold and frost. In the smaller backwaters and eddies of the river, the differing microclimates provide conditions for a huge variety of orchids, lichen, algae, mosses, ferns and mushrooms. Bubbling brooks meandering through peaty marshes and misty bogs could perhaps rival some of the best sources for Scottish single malts!

Blue sheep canter down steep inclines in the vicinity of Chomolhari.

Cultivable zones also vary with altitude and, as I climb higher through forests of silver oak and willow, I come upon an occasional clearing of apricot orchards and fields of amaranth and buckwheat. Villages and hamlets are fewer and farther between and the newcomer is a matter of innocent curiosity for the local people. Greetings are shyly exchanged, children wave playfully, and then suddenly someone offers me a handful of fruit. I wish I had something to give in return, but all that I can offer is a smile and heartfelt *kadinchhe*. It's difficult to match the warmth and spontaneity that comes through the dignified reserve of these mountain people. Late in the evening, as the sun dips quite suddenly behind the mountains, I reach Shamazampa, the first camp set in a flat stretch of land on the river bank. The climb is not very steep so far, but several stretches are rough, eroded by the stamping and scraping of boots and hooves, and the long hike begins to exact its toll on my knees. My entourage has lagged behind but before anxiety can seriously creep in, the mules and guides appear amidst a

92

jangling of bells and triumphant war whoops. In no time the camp gets going and the delightful smells of cooking on a wood fire fill the air.

That night it rained and I struggled with the cold and the wet while the crashing river vied with the thunderstorm beating a persistent tattoo against the canvas walls of my tent to drown out any vestige of sleep. But by morning, the rain gives way to crisp sunshine and it's good to get going again to shake off the chill. The landscape becomes increasingly spectacular as one climbs higher, especially the first sight, after three days' walk from Drugyel, of the snow-capped Chomolhari summit rising majestically above the river valley. While the fleeting sight of the mountain is inspiring, it's still another day to the Chomolhari base camp.

The last two days are a fairly stiff climb, while the atmosphere becomes increasingly

Yaks graze on Himalayan meadows.

rarefied with the gain in altitude. Thangthanka, a camp of colourful tents, beckons with a cup of hot salted tea, an excellent concoction for burning lungs and parched throats especially when it's topped off with a bit of smelly yak butter! The terrain changes imperceptibly at first. The firs are stunted and the forest sparse while dwarfed rhododendron shrubs roll down mountain-sides to the gurgling stream below. Patches of snow lie unmelted in the shade and wild yak graze on flower-bedecked Himalayan pastures. It takes a while to recognise that one has entered a different ecosystem beyond the tree line where an untamed landscape unfolds and icy winds whistle down from craggy cliffs, now speckled white from early winter snow.

This is a naturalist's paradise, land of the brilliantly coloured tragopan, the snow partridge, the high-flying lammergeyer, the elusive snow leopard, musk deer, blue

Following pages 94-95: *A morning glow bathes the summit of Chomolhari.*

93

sheep, Himalayan black bear and takin—Bhutan's national animal—as well as a host of herbal and medicinal plants and wild flowers. This is the heart of the Jigme Dorji National Park, a conservation area which spreads over 4,200 sq kms—one of the largest biosphere reserves in Asia.

In order to preserve the environmental sanctity of the mountains, no new settlements are permitted within the boundaries of the sanctuary. Yet several nomadic tribes inhabit the region herding yak and sheep, and traditionally barter livestock products—meat, hides, cheese and butter—with commodities from the valleys below. These Wang tribes people trace their ancestry to Mongol invaders and were called *Wangi Melo*—those who came and never left. Although the Wang were converted to Buddhism as far back as the mid-thirteenth century by Phajo Drukgom Shigpo, the ancient animist traditions of the *Bonpo* are still manifest in the reverence for natural divinities—mountains, forests, lakes and animals. This mix of identities is evident in the *chortens* made of ram's antlers, skulls of blue sheep, sprigs of sweet-smelling juniper and bristly pine cones—all topped with Buddhist prayer flags. Many religious dances and rituals performed by Buddhist monks in Bhutan and Tibet still bear animist origins. Interestingly enough, the Bhutanese crown is adorned by the black raven, considered to be the manifestation of Gonpo Jarodonchen, Mahakala with a raven's head, a powerful protective deity.

Jangothang appears suddenly. The track comes around a mountain spur, and there it is: Chomolhari! Shimmering in the late afternoon light, the great dome—24,000 ft high—turns from silver to gold and then glows white even in the darkness that follows. It's twelve degrees below freezing, at the Jangothang base camp 10,000 ft below the summit, but the spectacular view and the absolute serenity of the place engulfs one's senses. The place has a mystic charm heightened by the ruins of an old fortress above the icy stream rushing down from the melting glacier. Humbled in the presence of greatness, I spent the next couple of days watching and admiring the sublime beauty of the Goddess and learnt to appreciate her many moods which could alternate between peaceful and angry, welcoming and threatening in the space of a few minutes.

Late one evening, a flurry of activity shatters the peace as a herd of unruly yak, burdened with heavy saddles and adorned with gaily decorated headgear, enters the camp. Yelling and screaming, yak-herders struggle to get their steeds under control and bedded down for the night, but no one ever quite succeeds in disciplining this essentially wild beast. Save perhaps for the thoroughly intimidating dogs, cold-eyed and armed with sharp fangs—and reputed in the plains as the fearsome breed of Bhutias—which work all night long to make sure the yaks remain within their makeshift corral. Next morning, the loads are transferred to the yaks for the onward journey, while the mules turn back towards Drugyel unable to withstand the further rigours of this high terrain. But yaks are not the intelligent, sure-footed pack animals that mules have evolved to be. They balk at any move to load them or to move them and are quite apt to bolt down the mountain with their precious cargo and off-load it in the nearest stream! The convoy of yak got going later in the day, kicking and snorting, and triggered a minor stampede amongst the mules. Unfortunately I got caught in the melee, and although my photographic equipment survived, my arm went into a sling and my expedition into a tailspin back to civilisation. But memories of the high Himalaya, the sharp-edged pinnacle of Jichu Drakye and of the divine Chomolhari, remain imprinted on my mind forever. In some ways, like the *Wangi Melo*—the people who never left—I too seem to have left a part of myself in these mountains.